Living
in the
Giving

My HAE Story

© 2024 by Donna Kay Davis

All rights reserved.
This book or any portion thereof may not be reproduced or used in any manner whatsoever without the express written permission of the publisher except for the use of brief quotations in a book review.

Paperback ISBN: 9798822962781

Library of Congress Control Number: 2024915163

Living in the Giving
My HAE Story

A LOVING AND PASSIONATE
PATIENT ADVOCATE

Donna Kay Davis

Hereditary Angioedema

Mommy, My Face HURTS!

Kristian and Patrick's dad had already flown to Oahu, one of the seven inhabited Hawaiian Islands, prior to beginning our new air force assignment to Hickam Air Force Base, Hawaii. Our dear air force family friend JulieAnna needed to make a short-notice trip to St. Louis, Missouri, from where our families were staying in Little Rock, Arkansas. JulieAnna and her family were on their way to Ramstein AFB in Germany and needed to deliver their family car to Granite City, Illinois, for shipment to Germany. Great! Granite City was just eighteen miles from my mom and dad's house in St. Louis, Missouri. In keeping with "the air force way," we would without a second thought accompany our friend to drop off her car, take in the best of St. Louis, and enjoy one last visit with Oma and Opa prior to driving back to Little Rock, Arkansas, with JulieAnna.

During the Davis boys afternoon nap at Oma's, horseplay on the wood-sided waterbed resulted in a bumped, bruised, and slightly bloodied lower lip. We treated Kristian with ice and hugs and continued the afternoon routine. No sign of serious trauma. Early the next morning at about 4:00 a.m., I woke to Kris shaking me awake and saying, "Mommy, my face HURTS!" We went into the restroom, and when I turned the light on, I saw that Kristian's entire face was severely swollen, beyond recognition! The sight took my breath away as I tried not to scare him with my reaction.

How strange and scary. This was not the first time we'd seen these unexplained, random swellings on many different parts of Kristian's body. But this incident by far was the worst! After taking time to call the military health insurance to make sure we would be covered for an emergency room visit and *after* going through the drive-through to get coffee and breakfast, we arrived at a small community hospital in Florissant, Missouri. To this day, I think back in horror about how unalarmed I was and my lack of urgency in getting him to the hospital. As we were checking in, Kristian was starting with stridor, an abnormal, high-pitched breathing sound that precedes airway blockage. Yes, the swelling was in his throat too. We were rushed into a trauma room, and Kristian was treated for anaphylaxis—a severe, potentially life-threatening allergic reaction which can occur within seconds or minutes of exposure to something you're allergic to, such as peanuts or bee stings (it can also occur a half hour or longer after exposure). Anaphylaxis can be treated by an injection of epinephrine (adrenaline shot), Benadryl (an antihistamine), and a steroid called Solu-Medrol. Kris began the treatments immediately, but the customary speedy resolution did not come for him. In fact, the treatments had no effect on decreasing his swelling. The doctor checked on Kristian frequently and was prepared to intubate (to create a mechanical airway) if needed. During those check-ins, I began to share the many bizarre little swelling events we had seen Kris have since he was about two years old—on his foot one time, on his hand another time...or on his eyebrow. Even in his genital area. I remember thinking way back then...my God! What's next, his throat? We began bringing up the swelling during his well-baby checks. After an exhaustive investigation for allergies done by an immunologist at Little Rock Children's Hospital in Arkansas, we were told to "watch and document."

The tending physician came back into our room to tell us he normally did not do research in an emergency room environment, but he was going to take a little time for Kristian's case to gain a better understanding of what might be going on with Kristian. We learned that he was researching **hereditary angioedema (HAE)**. During this time in history, HAE was comprised of two to three sentences in medical textbooks. Our doctor ordered to have Kris transported to Barnes-Jewish Children's Hospital in St. Louis for some testing. To this day, I truly believe that what motivated this doctor to conduct his research was a God thing, aka, a miracle. I also learned that a few years before Kristian's miraculous diagnosis, there was a very small clinical trial conducted in the United States and published in the *New England Journal of Medicine* in the 1980s. This study tested the use of C1 esterase inhibitor by giving eleven doses in eight patients who had been diagnosed with hereditary angioedema (HAE). Perhaps this doctor had read through this journal edition and something about HAE remained in his consciousness.

"Hereditary angioedema is a rare, life-threatening, very painful "orphan" medical condition that affects every 1 in 10,000 to 1 in 50,000 individuals worldwide. It is a hereditary genetic defect. There are no boundaries regarding who could be affected by this condition. No geographic, ethnic, gender, or age predominance is found in HAE.[1]

---

[1]   https://www.haea.org/pages/p/what_is_hae

A Rare (Miraculous) Diagnosis for Our Five-Year-Old Son

Kristian's swelling gradually went down over the course of the next three days while he remained in the children's hospital. The pediatric allergist/immunologist ordered some blood tests, and on August 21, 1995, Kristian was diagnosed with a "textbook case" of hereditary angioedema as described below:

> Most cases of angioedema or swelling are not HAE or C1 esterase inhibitor deficiency.
>
> HAE is very rare, and most people—including medical professionals—are unfamiliar with the disease until they encounter someone who has it. Even then, as symptoms come and go, it is common for people with HAE to remain undiagnosed for many years. Frequent and severe abdominal pain can easily be misdiagnosed, sometimes even resulting in unnecessary exploratory surgery.
>
> Proper diagnosis is crucial for successful treatment and management of HAE. Laboratory analysis of blood samples, or genetic samples, are

required to establish an HAE diagnosis. There are three specific blood tests used to confirm hereditary angioedema type I or II:
1. C1-inhibitor quantitative (antigenic)
2. C1-inhibitor functional
3. C4.[2]

My mom and dad accompanied me to the diagnosis meeting, during which time the doctor told me Kristian has a very rare disease, one which he had never encountered before. The doctor went on to say Kris had a dysfunctional blood protein that kept his body's swelling process in check. This meant that any time he experienced things that would activate his immune system, like trauma, stress, illness, excitement—yes even excitement—he could have this uncontrollable swelling somewhere on his body. Now for the really bad news, he told us there were no medicines to treat or cure this condition here in the US. He went on to say he knew there was a therapy available in Europe and that the US may begin clinical trials to get a treatment FDA approved sometime in the near future. So, it would be my job to advocate for Kristian to participate in a clinical trial as soon as one became available. The doctor said Kristian must have access to this lifesaving treatment. The doctor also said that because this condition was hereditary, the rest of the immediate family should be tested. Wow! I was speechless, fear-stricken, and *confused*. How could Kris have this, with all the crazy swelling events, while nobody else in the family seemed

---

[2] https://www.haea.org/pages/p/what_is_hae#diagnosis

to have this problem? Later, we would learn that not only did Kris have this rare disease, but he was in a sub-category of patients (a 20 percent group of all those diagnosed with HAE) that had a sporadic gene mutation. Kris was confirmed to be a "de novo mutation—a genetic alteration that is present for the first time in one family."[3] The rest of our family tested negative. Kristian had a de novo hereditary angioedema, type II (dysfunctional C1 esterase inhibitor), diagnosis. Wow!

Kristian fully recovered from the swelling and was running all around the hospital ward with his brother Patrick. He was released from the hospital three days after he was admitted. We learned much later that HAE attacks left untreated usually resolved within three to four days.

---

3   NIH National Cancer Institute. https://www.cancer.gov/publications/dictionaries/cancer-terms/def/de-novo-mutation.

The HAE Pilgrimage

In keeping with human nature, I was desperate to learn as much as I possibly could before this pilgrimage into the great unknown of HAE. I only knew one person in the medical profession who might be willing and able to consult with me. Carol Dotson (Holmes) and I met in the second grade at Lusher Elementary School in Florissant, Missouri, twenty-five years prior. We became good friends. At the end of second grade, my family moved to my dad's childhood state of New Jersey and then returned to the same house in Florissant early in my fifth-grade year. Guess whose Lusher Elementary class I was placed into...Carol's class! Our friendship continues even today. At this time of great need for understanding, Carol, a practicing intensive care nurse, was able to help me understand a little more about the HAE physiology that was occurring in Kristian's body, enough to convince me that I *did* need to become Kristian's fearless advocate.

Our bags were packed, the household goods had already been shipped, and Daddy was already on the island working on finding housing and picking up the family car that was already shipped to our new home in Hawaii. In my follow-up with Tricare, our military insurance, regarding Kristian's hospitalization and ambulance ride, I learned that we would have to get approval from the military hospital in Hawaii before we could take Kristian to live on the island with this medical condition. The hospital would also need to have the capability of conducting clinical trials. We were less than a week out from our travel plans. Daddy would have to let his squadron commander know of this new development, and they would have to work quickly to get authorization to have Kristian treated at the Tripler Army Medical Center. The clock was ticking *loudly* as we waited for the approval. Finally, Dr. Aparna Shah, the chief of the Allergy and Immunology department, called and provided the authorization. We were to contact the clinic as soon as we arrived so that Dr. Shah could hopefully see Kristian before he had another swelling episode.

Getting Help for Kristian in Hawaii

Dr. Aparna Shah and Dr. Braden Shoupe, the pediatric hematology-oncologist at Tripler Army Medical Center, immediately began inquiring about a drug study and encouraged us to continue with our move to the island. They spent the next year and a half working on the audacious task of enrolling a young child into a drug study. Finally, on December 2, 1997, we received an "open label" clinical trial protocol and consent forms to sign. This consent was for Kristian to receive C1 esterase inhibitor (the blood protein enzyme that was dysfunctional in his blood) through participation in the C1 esterase inhibitor (human) IMMUNO open-label clinical trial, a clinical trial in which both the doctor and the patient know that the treatment is being given. The C1 esterase inhibitor used in the clinical trial had been successfully approved and used in Europe since 1979. Knowing this treatment had been safely and effectively used in Europe for eighteen years eased our minds in knowing the treatment outcome was not going to be a mystery.

Lifesaving Treatment Through Clinical Trial Participation

After signing the consent forms and anxiously waiting for the drug company to ship the blood product to the clinical trial site set up for Kristian at Tripler, we were informed that IMMUNO, the Italian drug company who originally sponsored the study, had been bought out by Baxter Healthcare Corporation in the US and they made changes to the clinical site requirements. It wasn't until November of 1999 that we learned from the Tripler Institutional Review Board that Baxter's new site requirements mandated that all nurse and physician study investigators be Hawaii State certified. At this juncture, Tripler could no longer be a study site, because military physicians and nurses did not get certified in the state or locations of their military assignments while working in military hospitals.

We were very fortunate and encouraged to learn that Dr. Shoupe was a longtime friend and colleague of Dr. Robert Wilkinson, lead of the Hematology and Oncology department of Kapiolani Medical Center for Women and Children in Hawaii. Dr. Shoupe contacted Dr. Wilkinson, aka Dr. Bob, on our behalf to see if he would be willing to take over as the physician investigator of this clinical trial for Kris. He agreed and immediately initiated an institutional review board at his facility. Finally, in June of 2000, we received the protocol and consent forms to sign. Kristian received his first dose of C1 esterase inhibitor in October of that year, which successfully stopped his severe facial swelling within a half hour. Prior to this first "miracle dose" and during the years of frustration and prayerful anticipation, Kristian endured countless painful and life-threatening runaway swelling episodes since arriving in Hawaii in 1995. He needed intensive care on three different occasions.

The Oahu Liquid Gold Years

C1 esterase inhibitor, an enzyme that is extracted and purified from whole blood, was like liquid gold for Kris. The duration of an untreated swelling attack is usually three to four days. Attacks in his abdomen caused excruciating pain, violent vomiting, and diarrhea. During abdominal attacks, the lining of the intestines would swell, which created a bowel obstruction. Kris would dry heave sometimes for up to eight hours, leaving him completely exhausted. All I could do was hold Kristian's forehead to keep his face from falling into the bowl. Kristian's abdominal attacks came on quick. So even during the clinical trial, usually by the time we arrived at the hospital for the treatment to be given, he was already experiencing all of the aforementioned symptoms. He would get the infusion that was administered over the course of ten minutes. After about fifteen minutes, we would watch the color come back to his very pale skin, he would start to get talkative, and within a half hour, he was up being a little boy and telling us how hungry he was. Liquid gold!

Aside from having to stay close to Kristian's clinical trial site, which meant we could not leave the island with him, we really did enjoy our lives in the Islands during this time. We lived on Hickam AFB, which was an amazing place for my two very active young boys to run and play with wide boundaries. The residential areas were under the watchful eyes of hundreds of stay-at-home spouses along with base security. The enforced speed limit through the housing area was 15 mph.

I too was able to enjoy the island even though the Hawaii Air National Guard (HIANG) kept the boys' dad primarily off the island, which was all part of an amazing air force flying career. I considered it an honor to support this career. The only requirement was for my spouse to bring home lots of pictures and stories. Meanwhile, the boys enjoyed endless water sport opportunities just as much as I did; we would sail, surf, paddle, and snorkel the days away when not in school or doing homework.

Our Life in the Air Force

I was born in St. Louis, Missouri, in 1961. I have an older sister, an older brother, and a younger brother eleven years younger than me. We had a good childhood together, with parents who stayed happily married until my father passed away with a treatable form of colon cancer due to his disdain for doctors. We were a happy family.

I married my spouse during his last year at Southeast Missouri State University (SEMO) when we were both twenty-one years old. We were happy to have one year of married life together at SEMO before we went off to his eight months of pilot training together in Phoenix, Arizona. With joyfulness and excitement, I set out to become the best supportive air force wife I could possibly be as we went on to a four-and-a-half-year tour in Japan followed by a three-year tour in Germany.

During our time in Japan, I completed my associate's degree in business from the University of Maryland's Global Campus at Yokota AFB near Tokyo. After I graduated, I was hired to work as an assistant manager for the University of Maryland textbook department.

I worked in a *very* busy office. We provided textbooks and managed shipments to twenty-nine campuses on eight-week terms in the Far East: Korea, Japan, Okinawa, Guam, Australia, Singapore, and Diego Garcia.

Toward the end of our assignment in Japan, I was able to take some time off before leaving the country. I enjoyed exploring the island and got to visit Korea, the Philippines, Guam, Thailand, and Hong Kong (while it was still a British territory). During this time off, I was also able to use the air force gymnasium on the military base to work off some of the weight I gained while going to school and working. I really enjoyed working out and realized an amazing physical transformation. Folks in the gym noticed and started asking me for help. I began to think, if I am going to be helping folks in the gym, I should have a better knowledge of how to promote safe exercise. By researching education that would support a career in the fitness industry, I learned that St. Louis University was interested in customizing a bachelor's degree designed for enabling me to become a leader in the emerging one-on-one training fitness industry. Perfect! A business/fitness education. I was SO excited! The stars were aligning for me to use my education and work while continuing to support my spouse's military career—nearly impossible for a military wife. My spouse was going to be away for six months training in the Philippines during this time. I could travel back to St. Louis, stay with my parents, and complete the coursework during the time he was going to be in the Philippines. We would then meet up in the St. Louis area, where he was scheduled to continue training at Scott Air Force Base in Illinois for his new VIP support flying assignment in Germany. I was shocked and very disappointed when my spouse said he would not allow me to go back to St. Louis early even though he was not going to be in Japan. He said that one of his fellow pilots warned him that if he let me leave early, I probably wouldn't remain with him going forward. In honor of our marriage, I did not go. The next best opportunity for me to continue my educational interest was to study and travel to Chicago, Illinois, for a weekend to sit for a certification exam. I used the exam objectives to guide my purchase of textbooks and was able to prepare myself for certification as a personal trainer through the National Academy of Sports Medicine (NASM).

We arrived in Germany in the early nineties. It was clear with the new language barrier; I would initially have to provide personal training on the military base. Learning to speak German would come with time. After settling into our new home in Homburg-Erbach, Germany, I began to reach out to different organizations on Ramstein Air Force Base to discuss the possibility for providing one-on-one fitness training in the base fitness center. I was told that Morale, Welfare, and Recreation programs were mission-sustaining programs for promoting physical and mental well-being for military members and their families. These programs were funded by congressional category A: mission-sustaining programs (unappropriated funds). I was told that there was no provision for my request and was encouraged to conduct a military community interest survey and submit a proposal for a personal services contract. Success! I was awarded the first ever personal services contract to provide one-on-one fitness instruction on a military base through Morale, Welfare, and Recreation.

I really enjoyed helping others—active-duty air force members, spouses, and student athletes (sons and daughters of active-duty members)—and did so for about a year. I became pregnant with my first child, Kristian, in February of 1991. I did have a challenging pregnancy. Just as I was finding out that I was expecting, the military hospital in Landstuhl, Germany, was closed to prepare for war casualties during the onset of the First Gulf War. I was switched to a German hospital, where the doctors spoke good English, but the nurses spoke next to none. Patrick, my second son, was conceived in Germany in 1993 and born one month after we arrived at our next air force assignment at Little Rock Air Force Base in Arkansas; we closed on our new home there just one week before Patrick was born. It was during this time when Kris began to have several bouts of unexplained swelling at just two years of age. Two more years would pass before our fateful trip with JulieAnna to St. Louis, when Kristian received his diagnosis.

The Liquid Gold Years and Becoming a Patient Advocate

I was able to pick up where I left off with my health and fitness career. I already knew how to get another personal services contract to do training on the Joint Base Pearl Harbor–Hickam military installations. Once again, I enjoyed providing instruction to the military community while the boys were in school. During this time, I was awarded a scholarship for continued education from Morale, Welfare, and Recreation and the Hickam Fitness Center. The monies were made available through the 1998 Master Settlement Agreement,

> ...the largest civil litigation settlement in US history. The 1998 Master Settlement Agreement between the major tobacco companies, forty-six US states, the District of Columbia, and five US territories transformed tobacco control. The states and territories scored a victory that resulted in the tobacco companies paying the states and territories billions of dollars in yearly installments. The money served as compensation for taxpayers' money that

had been spent in connection with tobacco-related diseases and the loss to local economies.[4]

My supervisor considered me to be a good candidate for a six-week intensive course offered on the island by the American College of Sports Medicine (ACSM). The health fitness instructor certification required academic, practical, and oral examination upon completion and enabled me to work with post-cardiac and post-orthopedic surgery patients under physicians' guidance.

I was getting a lot of referrals from my clients on base and had several people interested in my training off the military bases. My new ACSM credentials allowed me to take a master trainer position at one of the most exclusive fitness clubs on the island. While working in this new community, I realized I had a heart for working with the senior, post-cardiac, and post-orthopedic surgery club members under physician guidance. I did have one client ask if I could provide training for bodybuilding competitions, which was a good question. I knew I could academically, but not through experience. My friend and my mentor Rey Ronquilio, titled Mr. USA (Lightweight) 2003 and National Master's Lightweight 2002, agreed to train me to compete in the 2002 US Armed Forces bodybuilding competition in Hawaii. I was titled second in the Ladies' Lightweight division. Not bad for an air force wife, mom, and fitness instructor.

---

4   Truth Initiative. "Inspiring Lives Free From Smoking, Vainglorious & Nicotine." https://truthinitiative.org/who-we-are/our-history/master-settlement-agreement

As we continued to enjoy our life in Hawaii, we were beginning to anticipate the end of the clinical trial participation for Kris and FDA approval of the treatment that worked so well for him. It was during this time that we got called into the hospital for a meeting regarding the clinical trial. We were told that the study would go on hold while the study sponsor, Baxter Healthcare Corporation, redesigned the protocol. Another year had lapsed as we endured, once again, Kristian's untreated HAE attacks. At the end of that year, we learned the new protocol would have to show safety and efficacy in one hour. The original protocol and all other protocols that garnered approval of the treatment in Europe had a four-hour window for showing safety and efficacy. The problem with the one-hour window for showing safety and efficacy was as follows: At one hour, the patients who got the medicine and the patient who did not get the medicine did not show significant enough differences to garner FDA approval. If the two patients were compared at four hours, those untreated would progress to having a very severe HAE attack, or in some cases, death. Those that did get treated with the medicine would be back to carrying on their lives as if nothing ever happened. Our physician investigators (leading physician experts for hereditary angioedema here in the US who were conducting our clinical trials) were incensed and protested that this change would more than likely cause the study to fail. They pleaded with Baxter to reconsider, because failure of this study could result in patient deaths while waiting for another clinical trial to become available. The protocol *did* end up failing, and this medicine that proved to work so well in the clinic for Kris and other HAE patients was *not* FDA approved. Once again, it was also during this time that Kristian's attacks became more frequent and much more severe. Once again, Kristian's life was filled with fear, pain, academic failure, and missed social opportunities. He was having two to three back-to-back attacks a week that would each last between two to four days, resulting in complete disability for this young boy. Given the frequent and dangerous nature of our son's attacks, we had no choice but to take our pediatrician's advice to start him on a three-times-a-day dose of Oxandrolone, a high dose of anabolic steroid. During this time, Major League ballplayers, bodybuilders, and other professional athletes were getting arrested for the use of anabolic steroids, and these medicines have always been contraindicated for women and children. Kris was just nine years old at the time. Anabolic steroids increase the production of C1 esterase inhibitor in the liver at the expense of some very serious side effects, including cancer. Additionally, it became obvious that not even this extreme effort to provide relief for Kris worked. He continued to have the same attack frequency and severity while on the anabolic steroid. Patrick was also significantly and negatively affected by HAE. With the boy's father so frequently off the island and with no family nearby for support, there was no other option other than all three of us heading to the hospital to combat the HAE attacks. Friends can only help so much at 3:00 a.m. and all other times of day and night.

Patient Advocacy

It was clear I needed to be a patient advocate. My spouse's military flying career, the boys' schooling, and Kristian's life would be dependent on how quickly Kristian could regain access to the liquid gold.

The military flying career usually starts to wind down and families start to anticipate retirement right around the twenty-year point. Ours extended to twenty-three years. Pilots who continue in the military beyond flying move on to higher ranks and leadership positions. For those who retire, commercial flying usually comes into focus. The transition is not easy. A military pilot would have to keep their flying credentials current, unless they were independently wealthy and could afford the very expensive requalification and ratings required to fly commercially. Also, the first year with an airline is considered a probation, and families must prepare for getting paid about one-third of the military salary at retirement. For our military retirement, the plan was for me to step up my financial contribution to the family to make the transition.

The military did offer a resource for families who were struggling with catastrophic events on the home front. The program was called the Exceptional Family Member Program (EFMP). This program considered the needs of the family and made adjustments for the active-duty member in order to accommodate the special needs of the family. In our case, the boys' father would have to give up his flying status. This would surely be a nail in the coffin and death to a commercial flying career after the military for my spouse. To preserve that opportunity for the family, I chose to carry the responsibility on the home front and did not ask for EFMP help from my spouse or the military.

Schooling on the island was a challenge unto itself. Sadly, there was a fair amount of stigma for Caucasian children on the island, especially for boys. There was also a fair amount of disdain for military families in the local communities, so putting the boys into local public schools was risky. The Department of Defense (DOD) schools on the military base were small with limited resources. With both boys missing so much school due to constant inpatient stays for Kris in the hospital and the insufficiency of the DOD school resources for accommodating special needs children, we had no choice other than to put the boys into costly private schools. The Lutheran school system turned out to be a godsend for our family.

The next attack could be the laryngeal (throat) swelling attack that could take Kristian's life. It was clear the loss of treatment through the clinical trial for Kris made it impossible for me to provide motivation to others as a health fitness instructor.

Has There Ever Been a Good Time to Have Hereditary Angioedema?

During this period of Kristian's life, I would have said, "Hell NO!" But years later, I did realize the time was ripe for me to successfully advocate for my son and soon joined other HAE patients here in the US that would form the US Hereditary Angioedema Association (HAEA).

There were two major milestones during this time in our country's history that laid the path for us to begin our journey:
1. The passing of HR 5238, which became the Orphan Drug Act of 1983
2. Widespread availability of the internet

The Passing of HR 5238, Which Became the Orphan Drug Act of 1983

Dr. John Swann, FDA historian, explains so eloquently what I needed to communicate regarding how this powerful legislation opened the door for hereditary angioedema advocacy:

> Scientific developments throughout the twentieth century led to the development of many medical products and therapeutic advances for patients. But around the late 1970s, it became increasingly clear that many citizens were being left out of these advances. One of the key reasons for this neglect was the small size of some patient populations. The relatively limited prevalence of a particular disease acted as a barrier for commercial investment in the research and development required to show evidence of the safety and efficacy of treatments. Ironically, by the early 1980s, these "rare diseases" affected 20–25 million patients who, together, suffered from approximately 5,000 rare diseases—some of which affected as few as about a dozen individuals.

In response, organizations were established in the Department of Health and Human Services and in [the] FDA (the Office of Orphan Products Development) to promote the development of products to treat these "orphan" diseases. At least as important was the grassroots efforts of patients and advocates affected by such rare diseases as Gaucher's disease, Tourette's syndrome, Huntington's disease, severe combined immunodeficiency (SCID), and many other disorders. They formed a coalition in the early 1980s, which evolved into the National Organization for Rare Disorders (NORD), and which led in 1983 to the enactment of the Orphan Drug Act. As Abbey Meyers, the head of the organization and the mother of a Tourette's syndrome patient, later noted, "We look back on this adventure with a great sense of accomplishment and relief. It was an opportunity for patients with rare diseases to empower themselves. I doubt if we would have [had] such an effective and cohesive group if we had not faced opposition at every turn."

The Orphan Drug Act provided financial incentives to attract [the] industry's interest through a seven-year period of market exclusivity for a drug approved to treat an orphan disease, even if it were not under patent, and tax credits of up to 50 percent for research and development expenses. In addition, [the] FDA was authorized to designate drugs and biologics for orphan status (the first step to getting orphan development incentives). The FDA also provided grants for clinical testing of orphan products and offer assistance in how to frame protocols for investigations. A subsequent amendment defined a rare disease as one affecting under 200,000, though a disease with more patients could qualify if the firm could not recover the costs of developing the drug.

The 1983 Orphan Drug Act completely changed the face of therapeutics for rare disorders. By 1990, [the] FDA had designated 370 products for orphan status, and of these, forty-nine were approved for orphan indications. By 2002, the number of orphan designations grew to almost 1,100 and approvals to 232, a number that provided treatment to an estimated 11 million patients. Much work of course remained to be done, considering how many suffered from rare disorders. But the Orphan Drug Act finally provided for many of those orphaned among blockbuster treatments a hope of their own thanks to the work of many, not the least of whom were those patients and their advocates who had long championed the needs of the forgotten patients.[5]

---

5   John Swann, PhD, FDA historian. https://www.fda.gov/industry/fdas-rare-disease-day/story-behind-orphan-drug-act

Widespread Availability of the Internet

"The internet emerged in the United States in the 1970s but did not become visible to the general public until the early 1990s."[6] The internet really DID revolutionize our lives in countless ways and allowed our individual communities to become united communities across the country. People with like interests were able to join together in groups with others across the US and throughout the world. Yahoo, which stands for "yet another hierarchical officious oracle," is a communication platform and was one of the first internet group platforms that became available to anyone with access to a computer at no cost in January 2001. Without the advancements shared in this little history lesson, Kristian and other patients like him would have faced a life filled with unimaginable pain, disability, and possibly even death due to HAE.

---

6   Summarized from Britannica.

"I Have HAE Swelling, Do You?"

Soon after Yahoo Groups became available, a father from Hershey, Pennsylvania, who had HAE and who passed the condition to his child started a Yahoo Group and simply posed the question, "I have HAE swelling. Do you?" Following that inquiry and filled with hope of getting to know others who had HAE swelling, a small group of patients joined together from across the US and began to develop deep friendships, support, and camaraderie. I, too, found this group and started communicating with other patients. Having this opportunity was invaluable to our family since Kristian was the only one in our family with this condition. The information I could get from other parents and patients helped me immensely while taking care of Kristian.

Advocating for Kris and HAE in Hawaii — The HIANG 204th Airlift Squadron

Our family will be forever grateful for the men and women of the 204th Airlift Squadron on Hickam Air Force Base for their assistance and concern for our family. There were members of the squadron who had connections to our Hawaii congressional representatives. Diane Knight, married to one of the squadron members, was a nurse and had worked with a medical staffer for Senator Daniel Inouye. She encouraged me to reach out to the staffer, knowing that sometimes congressional representatives can help their constituents. US Air Force General Walt Kaneakua was also very helpful in getting our medical concern about the failed clinical trial heard by Senator Inouye. The outreach from Ms. Knight and General Kaneakua led to me communicating directly with the staff nurse in the senator's office in Washington, DC, who proved to be very helpful for Kris and later for the Hereditary Angioedema Association.

Fighting for Our Children's Lives

The HAE Yahoo group very quickly became the lifeline for HAE patients and their families. I had mentioned in the Yahoo group that I was communicating with Senator Inouye's office. I was encouraged by the members of the group to reach out to a particular HAE patient who suffered along with both of his daughters. This gentleman lived in the Washington, DC, area and held a high-level position in the US Federal Reserve. His family, like ours, was devastated by the clinical trial failures. His oldest daughter and Kris were two of the most severely affected children in the HAE group. I did communicate with him about Senator Inouye. He in turn told me that the National Organization for Rare Disease (NORD) was having a conference for rare disease patients and other rare disease stakeholders. He encouraged me to contact NORD and try to attend. He went on to say that a group of HAE patients would be attending the meeting to begin the process of organizing as a national patient organization. Kristian and I were able to attend, and I became one of the original members of the US Hereditary Angioedema Association (HAEA) along with the gentleman from DC and several others.

Honolulu (HNL) to Washington Dulles/DC (IAD)

Kris was in his stroller alongside me as we waited for boarding to begin at Honolulu International Airport for our flight to the DC area for the NORD conference. Just as we were called to board the flight, he vomited. Was it my worst fear—Kris has an attack on the flight—or was he just excited...or both? It was a tough decision whether to walk back off the flight or not. We did stay on the flight, and sure enough, Kris was having an abdominal attack. He proceeded to vomit and dry heave for a large portion of the flight. By the time we arrived in DC the next morning, he had soiled everything we had onboard with us for him except for his winter coat and one pair of blue jeans. We even had to put the lining of his car seat into a plastic bag.

As we walked into the hotel lobby, we were greeted by one of the hosts for the NORD organization conference. During our warm and personal welcome, the host looked across the lobby and said, "Oh, there's someone I would like you to meet." She walked us over to a very distinguished-looking man in a business suit and tie. She introduced us to Dr. Eric Phillips, a neurologist from Nebraska. The host told the doctor that Kristian was an HAE patient who had just arrived from Hawaii. Dr. Phillips got down on one knee and took Kristian's hands into his. With tears welling up in Dr. Phillip's eyes, he said, "You are the first person I've ever met outside my family who has HAE." He was there for the NORD conference too...as a patient.

We got a phone call from a NORD staff member the following day asking if they could do an interview with Kris for their NORD magazine. I agreed. Kris was napping all afternoon. He was completely exhausted from the twelve hours of travel and his horrendous HAE abdominal attack during the flight. When it came time for the interview, I could not get Kris to get dressed. He wanted to go back to sleep. The reporter came to our hotel room a little later in the day and conducted the interview there.

The time at the conference flew by. We had a couple meetings as a group of HAE patients and then signed up to be members of the Hereditary Angioedema Association.

The Hereditary Angioedema Association and the Orphan Drug Act

Our Orphan Drug Act grassroots effort went from zero to max effort after our NORD meeting. The one and only clinical trial which was saving the lives of our children had tragically failed. The president of the HAEA had already been in communication with the FDA and others involved in advocating for rare disease nationally and internationally. In recognition of the life-threatening, unmet medical need of HAE patients, the FDA conveyed to Baxter Healthcare (the sponsor of the failed study) that they would be allowed to provide continued treatment for HAE attacks to patients enrolled in the study until another clinical trial became available. Baxter wasted no time in telling HAE patients and the FDA that they were not willing to continue treating patients with HAE. Why?!

The HAEA president, the FDA, and others were able to get Baxter to agree to allow patients to use up what treatments remained in the study sites. Once the treatments were used up, sites would be closed. When we had gotten news about the study failure, we were made aware that there were seven treatments left in Kristian's site. It wasn't until we showed up to the site for a treatment that we learned that the C1 esterase inhibitor was packed up and shipped unrefrigerated back to Baxter on the mainland, which resulted in the destruction of the treatment promised for Kris that kept him safe. We were devastated. I reached out to our new friend Dr. Phillips and learned the same thing had happened at his clinical trial site.

A "Simple" Legal Question

It had been a while since I had talked to JulieAnna. She and her family lived in Reno, Nevada, at the time. Last time I touched base, I learned she had resumed her legal work since returning to the US. I reached out to her, as she was a friend and lawyer who knew of Kristian's condition. I had learned from the HAEA president that there was an email communication stating that Baxter would leave the medicine in the clinics to be used up. I called Julianna to ask a simple legal question: Could a promise made in an email communication be upheld in a court of law? I then went on to explain to her what had been going on for Kris. She could tell how upset I was and was so gracious to actually answer my question. She said right up front, "Donna, there is no such thing as a simple legal question." Out of love and concern for Kris, she did provide her legal perspective. She would not have done so for anyone else. After hearing what had happened, Julianna said there should be a Temporary Restraining Order (TRO) to address the action taken by Baxter.

JulieAnna learned from a legal peer in Hawaii that the jurisdiction covering a TRO filed for Kris would have to be filed in the United States District Court for the Eastern District of California in Sacramento, California. As if it had been orchestrated, surely a God thing, JulieAnna was licensed to practice law in California. Within two days, JulieAnna had created a TRO, which needed to be signed. It turned out that Kristian's father had an unscheduled flight which had him resting overnight in Reno, Nevada. He could sign the TRO!

Since I was now part of the HAEA, I did communicate with our president regarding the TRO. He told me he was aware of what happened at Kristian and Dr. Phillip's sites and learned of other sites that were closed with medicine taken away. He went on to say that he knew taking care of Kristian was my top priority. He said the association could not be involved in any legal proceedings for Kris or anyone else. I had already started doing volunteer work for the HAEA and knew that the efforts of the association were to identify HAE patients in the US as quickly as possible so that we could convince investors and pharmaceutical companies to do clinical trials for us. I agreed with the president that we could not appear to be a litigating patient organization at the same time we pursued clinical trials. No class action lawsuit!

My dear friend JulieAnna took Kristian's lawsuit on a pro bono basis. As a matter of fact, she pretty much gave up her life while the case was in progress. I do know she was sickened by what Baxter had done and wanted justice! No dollar amount could ever be enough for the time, effort, and concern JulieAnna showed for Kris.

DRUG COMPANY SETTLES BOY'S SUIT
By Denny Walsh, *Bee* Staff Writer

A Sacramento federal judge on Monday approved a confidential settlement between one of the world's largest pharmaceutical firms and an eleven-year-old boy who has depended on an experimental drug to treat his rare and potentially fatal disease.

Neither side would discuss the settlement's terms, but JulieAnna Anastassatos and Michael Rounds, the Reno attorneys who represent the boy and his parents, said their clients were "satisfied" with the outcome of the legal face-off with Baxter Healthcare Corp.

Kristian Davis is one of the few people in the world afflicted with hereditary angioedema, a genetic disorder characterized by recurrent and severe swelling of soft tissue. It results from a deficiency of a blood factor that inhibits swelling and appears to be triggered by stress.

Baxter Healthcare, an Illinois-based, multi-billion-dollar company, shut down study sites and destroyed unused portions of the serum called C1 esterase inhibitor, saying it did not prove effective enough to be licensed by the US Food and Drug Administration. The serum has long been available in Europe but is not approved for use in the United States.

But the attorneys for Kristian and his parents presented enough evidence of the drug's positive effect on the boy to persuade US District Judge

Lawrence K. Karlton to halt removal of the serum from a study site in Hawaii, where the family lives.

The temporary restraining order was issued in December. Kristian's attorneys then filed an amended complaint asking Karlton to permanently bar removal of the drug and closure of the study site in Honolulu. They also asked for an order requiring Baxter Healthcare to provide Kristian with the C1 blood product until it is approved by the FDA or becomes commercially available.

In January, Kristian's attorneys sought a preliminary injunction to keep the Hawaii study site open and the serum available until the case could be decided on the merits.

Karlton had not yet ruled on the injunction request when attorneys for both sides filed a motion last month asking the judge to approve the confidential settlement.

"This settlement agreement is fair to Kristian Davis and should be approved by the court," the motion states.

On Monday, with Kristian and his family in the courtroom, Karlton gave the pact his blessing.

First Paid HAEA Staff Member

Our president worked feverishly, spending countless hours in medical libraries and communicating with other rare disease organization leaders and the FDA. He put together presentations given to investors, pharmaceutical companies, congressional leaders, and other industry stakeholders. He proposed that investigational new drugs could be developed and used in small clinical trials for treating HAE attacks with possible applications for treating more prevalent medical conditions after garnering FDA approval. The benefit given through the Orphan Drug Act was a bonus. Four pharmaceutical companies in the six months left of that year committed to doing clinical trials for us.

I had been communicating my ongoing advocacy for Kris with the patient group. I did get invited to meet with Senator Inouye's staff in DC, who were very concerned about the outcome for Kris and other HAE patients. Once I had learned that the C1 esterase inhibitor Kris was getting in the clinical trial would not be FDA approved, I took a video in the clinic of Kris presenting for treatment with one of his horrendous abdominal attacks. I documented him going from violent illness to returning back to his hungry, talkative, playful self within a half hour after receiving the treatment. I shared that video with the HAEA president. The video was a very profound testament to the effectiveness of C1 esterase inhibitor.

The volunteer work I was doing for the HAEA had become almost a full-time job. I got a call from the president. He asked me what the association would have to pay for me to give up time spent doing fitness instruction to become the first paid staff member of the HAEA. I was offered a full-time position at a rate moderately above the amount I was able to earn as an instructor. With the demands of taking care of Kristian during his loss of access to HAE therapy, single parenting with the boys' father off the island so much, and the patient advocacy I was doing for Kris and the patient group, I was gaining weight along with losing the ability to keep up with my own high level of fitness and instructing others. Becoming the first HAEA paid staff member was good for me, Kris, our family finances, and the HAEA. I did consult with my spouse prior to accepting the offer. He had already been growing disenchanted with me. I was being pulled away from the idyllic life he had envisioned for us. He was not coping well with the change an HAE diagnosis brings to a family. He was not happy with the thought of me moving away from the fitness industry and begrudgingly allowed me to take the position with the HAEA.

During those years, I also played competitive softball with the Hawaii National Guard Squadron women's softball team. The team held the championship title for several years in a row. Due to increased flying demands on the squadron, forfeits due to not enough players was an issue. During this particular year, I told the team not to call me during the ongoing season because I was not conditioned to play at that competitive level. They did not call me until they were about to lose the championship due to a not-enough-players forfeit. The girls on the team and my spouse begged me to play. I did. During the second-to-last game of the championship, I actually got a stand-up double. In this league, those that didn't hit a home run usually got thrown out. During my advance to third base, I broke my stride to avoid being tagged and destroyed my knee by completely tearing my anterior cruciate ligament (ACL) along with meniscus damage. It was strange. I could walk, and there was not a whole lot of pain. My spouse was off island at the time, and the boys were with a sitter. After the game, I thought a couple of beers would taste good, so I went to the convenience store on base to buy the beer. While standing in the checkout line, I was wondering how bad I had hurt my knee. I moved my leg from side to side and almost fell over. Off to the emergency room! I drove to Tripler Army Medical Center. After drinking the two beers in the parking lot, I checked in and learned that I would be needing surgery if I wanted to continue keeping a moderate fitness level. I found it very interesting that the military was doing a clinical trial to study repairing an ACL prior to the initial healing from the injury. It was customary at the time to have patients heal, go through physical therapy to build strength, and then do the surgery. The doctor asked if I wanted to participate. Sounded good to me! I said yes and was asked to pick from a bunch of sealed envelopes to be randomly chosen or not. If I picked the envelope to participate, I would be having this major surgery in two days. I got lucky and chose an envelope that would randomize me into the study. My spouse would be home by then.

Building the HAE Association (HAEA)

The HAEA president had already booked his trip to the island prior to my softball accident. He arrived on the island about a week after my surgery. The trip was scheduled so we could begin to put together a process for helping the four pharmaceutical companies find patients for their studies. At that time, the HAE Yahoo Group had approximately 230 HAE sufferers and family members communicating with each other. Because HAE is a hereditary condition, each person with HAE could possibly have one, two, or more additional family members who may or may not be diagnosed or having symptoms. There could be even more affected family members in the extended families. We knew from our own family experiences that many in our families were undiagnosed. We would need to create a process for helping potential HAE patients get diagnosed in addition to getting patients into clinical trials. Our first work session in 2005 was "low tech." It consisted of a critical thinking exercise regarding what we needed to accomplish first. Our ideas were written down on a yellow legal pad. Toward the end of the session, we created a spreadsheet with the names, locations, and numbers of affected family members that we knew of from our friends in the HAE Yahoo Group. This would later become a relational database and ultimately turned into the US HAEA database, which currently has 10,000-plus patients registered. My first official task was to reach out to the individuals in the HAE Yahoo Group to communicate what we were doing and to invite them to participate.

New Clinical Trial Sites

Each one of the four clinical trials in the design process would need approximately one hundred HAE patient participants. I worked to identify hospitals in proximity to the HAE patients we knew of that could possibly become clinical trial sites. I worked with our members in order to reach out to their physicians who might be good clinical trial investigators. When we could not identify an HAE-treating physician through our patient group, I would research and cold call physicians doing other clinical trials near our patients. To my surprise, we did end up creating clinical trial sites through this method.

For the patients to regain access to therapy by participating in clinical trials and for pharmaceutical companies who expressed interest in doing HAE clinical trials, the race was on! During this time, the larger pharmaceutical companies interested in HAE clinical trials were successful in clinical trials and providing medications for the masses but were not as accustomed to working with patient advocacy groups and small patient populations. A synergy between a pharmaceutical company clinical trial sponsor and a patient advocacy group proved to be instrumental in conducting clinical trials for rare disease. Newly developed, Lev Pharmaceutical expressed interest in coordinating with the HAEA for identifying areas of the country needing clinical trials. They worked hand-in-hand with the HAEA right up to the end process of HAE patients testifying before the drug approval committees prior to FDA approval. Lev Pharmaceutical was a "bio-pharmaceutical company focused on developing and commercializing therapeutic products for the treatment of inflammatory diseases."[7]

Dr. Ira Kalfus and Jason Bablak led the HAE clinical trial effort for Lev Pharmaceutical. They spent countless hours on the phone with me as they worked to prepare the locations we identified as potential clinical trial sites. Their effort and willingness to work with the HAEA proved to be very successful. There were forty Lev Pharmaceutical clinical trial sites treating HAE patients by the end of that year. After completing and collecting the required safety and efficacy data, Lev Pharmaceutical was the first to garner FDA approval for use of C1 esterase inhibitor for treating hereditary angioedema attacks in 2009.

---

[7] https://www.bloomberg.com/profile/company/LEVP:US

Staffing the HAEA

Tom Moran said, "We need one hundred Donnas!"

Tom Moran worked closely with the president of the HAEA in the beginning. Tom provided consultation for the HAEA. The HAEA was able to draw from his experience as president of the Immune Deficiency Foundation and president of Primary Immune Services, Inc., from 2003 to 2006. Tom was a thought leader in nonprofit organization fundraising and also provided guidance in developing legislative and public education programs.

In the early days of the HAEA, funding for the organization was provided by HAE industry stakeholders (study sponsors, physician groups, access program developers, etc.). They provided educational grants for us to educate HAE sufferers on how important it was to get diagnosed and how important it was to have their other family members who were suffering to also get diagnosed.

We determined that the best way to accomplish what we needed to do as an organization was to identify HAEA patients and caregivers for immediate family members affected by HAE in our membership to help and potentially become paid staff members. The plan was to hire these individuals to create an HAEA patient services team. The president and I started searching for those people in our group. When we identified candidates, we conducted interviews, and then I would either travel to their home or the individual would fly to Hawaii for the two to three days of training I would carry out with the new hire. At this time, my boys were too young for me to be away for more than a day or two. Since traveling off the island and back required four to five days, most of the training was done in Hawaii. During my time with the HAEA, I hired and trained ten HAE patients/caregivers who selflessly helped to fill the need for the one hundred Donnas. I provided mentoring and supervision and remained on call for this new HAEA patient services team in these early days and for the next ten years. With all that needed to be done that involved me, working with the new patient services team, and the many organizational planning meetings, our president and our newly established board of directors decided to establish the HAEA, Inc., headquarters in Honolulu, Hawaii.

Growing the Database

In addition to the patient services team, another HAE patient/HAE mom from Georgia was very talented in all things related to information technology. She managed our database and never complained about our sometimes-daily requests for the database to accommodate a new task that we needed to be able to do as soon as possible.

There was a sense of urgency to get the physicians treating our current HAE patients who were willing to help other HAE patients into a "Physician Referral" part of our database. We needed to refer patients to HAE-knowledgeable physicians for getting diagnosed. In addition to this physician database, the HAEA was very fortunate to have several compassionate and generous expert physicians/scientists who offered their time and expertise to help our patient services team and HAE patients experiencing emergencies.

Worthy of Sainthood

Our HAEA patient services staff of seven individuals at the time served our growing patient community in a way worthy of sainthood. Each member of our team brought unique insights regarding the many challenges HAE patients faced in living with this condition. We would refer patients to a particular staff member who had knowledge of what the patient was experiencing. I can't remember one request for help that could not be addressed with personal experience and insight by one of our team members.

We realized right away that patients needed to have access to our help and HAEA resources day and night. We were able to establish a 24-7 emergency call line. It was not uncommon for patients who were traveling to end up needing help during swelling emergencies. In addition to our physician database, we had developed a database of hospitals that routinely treated other HAE patients. Following is an example of an emergency call we would encounter and how we helped:

A patient who was experiencing a throat attack and already having trouble talking would call the emergency line and hand the phone over to the ambulance staff. We would explain that the patient's throat swelling was due to an HAE swelling attack and that the treatments for anaphylaxis would not result in a positive outcome. We would find out what hospital the patient was being transported to and then call ahead of the patient's arrival to that hospital. We would let the emergency department know that the patient would be arriving with throat swelling due to hereditary angioedema. We offered to put the medical staff in contact with one of our on-call HAE physician experts who could provide peer-to-peer guidance on how best to manage the patient.

Each of our team members would do a twenty-four-hour on-call shift. It was my responsibility as the supervisor of this team to be available anytime day or night, should our emergency on-call person encounter a situation they were not comfortable in managing. The time difference between the East Coast of the US and Honolulu was six hours. When working on the island, my day started at 3:00 a.m., which was 9:00 a.m. on the East Coast. Incoming calls would begin to slow down around 10:00 or 11:00 am. I would take a short nap and then manage to get through the rest of the Hawaii day. My bedtime was 10:00 p.m. Honolulu time. I was remarkably able to keep up with the boys' school and sports schedules and always got nice meals on the table. To this day, the boys and their island friends still mention their favorite meals prepared by "Donna Mama."

High-Octane Stress Overload

While the Lev Pharmaceutical open-label clinical trial was ongoing, production of the C1 esterase inhibitor was halted, which created a shortage of the blood product used in the study. The HAEA was able to work with the FDA to keep *another* clinical trial from failing.

We learned that the FDA allows patients to personally import medications not FDA approved when there is no other treatment available to treat a medical condition and when that condition is life-threatening. HAE patients met both of these criteria. Our HAEA president had already made connections in Europe when his daughter, like Kris, lost access to C1 esterase inhibitor. He and other stakeholders were able to establish an alternative source of therapy by working with Sanquin in the Netherlands. Sanquin was established in 1998 through a merger between the Dutch blood bank and the central laboratory of the Netherlands Red Cross Blood Transfusion Service (CLB).[8] The HAEA was able

---

8 https://www.sanquin.nl/en/about-sanquin/the-story-of-sanquin

to expeditiously create a personal importation program which would help patients who were participating in the Lev Pharmaceutical study to personally import CETOR, Sanquin's C1 esterase inhibitor treatment. In addition to managing the patient services staff, I was tasked to manage special projects, and the personal importation program fell into my hands. By far, managing this task of helping twenty-three study patients personally import their monthly supply of CETOR was the most difficult and stressful time of my life. Kristian was one of those patients. My job was to help patients collect the documents required to import their needed C1 esterase inhibitor. The patients needed to have a physician willing to be identified as the managing physician for the imported treatment.

I realized very quickly that a lot of what I learned many years prior while managing the textbook department in the Far East came in handy and indeed made me the right person for the task. This effort proved to be very high stakes. It did not take long for the HAEA president and I to end up having direct contact with the director of the Office of Compliance and Biologics Quality (CBER, FDA). Each month went by *very* quickly. As soon as the patients submitted the paperwork for their personal importation from Sanquin, we would begin frantically getting everyone's paperwork and requests for personal importation completed for the next month. The preparation for the next month was frequently interrupted by the blood product that needed to be shipped and kept refrigerated getting embargoed at the US point of entry, which was the Federal Express Customs Clearance location in Memphis, Tennessee. In many of the embargo events, I could explain the nature of the importation and the shipment would be released right away. There were, however, several unnerving embargo events that required me to call the director of CBER, FDA, for assistance in getting the medication released. Sadly, we did lose a few months' supply shipments that perished. The product perished during the embargo delays, resulting in the product arriving warm due to the expiration of the ice packs in the shipping containers. Perishable medications shipped from the Netherlands to the US had a very short window for success. That familiar feeling of panic comes back to me even as I write about this project many years later.

CETOR at Home Compared to Many Hours Too Late in the Clinic

One of the physicians/scientists conducting the Lev Pharmaceutical clinical trial, the president of the HAEA, and HAE patients knew all too well that the time lapse between the beginning of an HAE attack and getting treated in a clinic was much too long. In this period of time, attacks usually progressed to the level of very severe or even life-threatening. The personal importation of CETOR opened the door to study and make a case for patients learning to infuse their treatment at home as soon as they realized they were having an attack. The HAEA capability to design and lay the groundwork for a study was primed for action. It did not take long to begin the "Safety and Efficacy of Physician-Supervised Self-Managed C1 Inhibitor Replacement Therapy" conducted by Louanne M. Tourangeau, Anthony J. Castaldo, Donna K. Davis, James Koziol, Sandra C. Christiansen and Bruce L. Zuraw." C1 inhibitor (C1INH) has recently been approved in the USA for the treatment of acute attacks in hereditary angioedema (HAE) patients. The literature suggests that treatment with

C1INH is most effective when administered early in an attack. Home infusion of C1INH allows for the earliest possible intervention since patients can initiate therapy at the first sign of symptoms.

Method: We performed an observational, prospective study on thirty-nine subjects with HAE utilizing two groups of patients: one receiving on-demand C1INH replacement therapy in a medical facility and the other self-managing on-demand C1INH replacement therapy in the home setting under the supervision of a treating physician. All subjects completed online questionnaires weekly for eight weeks.

Results: There were statistically significant decreases in attack duration ($p < 0.0001$), pain medication use ($p < 0.0001$) and graded attack severity ($p < 0.005$) in the subjects who received C1INH in the home setting versus the clinic-based group. Attack frequency was similar between the groups. The home group experienced more frequent injection-related side effects; however, the clinic group noted more severe adverse events from C1INH.

Conclusion: Physician-supervised self-managed C1INH replacement therapy is a safe and effective treatment for patients with HAE with potential benefits in diminishing attack duration and attack severity.[9] This study opened the door for patients to self-infuse FDA-approved C1 esterase inhibitor.

---

[9] International Archive of Allergy Immunology (March 2012), 157(4): 417–424. Published online November 25, 2011. doi: 10.1159/000329635
PMCID: PMC3242706

My Hand in Research

Throughout the next several years, I continued to be involved in the research efforts of the HAEA. The HAEA continued to promote research to improve the quality of life for HAE patients as an invaluable partner with many different HAE stakeholders. I spent countless hours involved in the design process of the patient outcomes and quality of life surveys used in this research. I also worked along with the institutional review boards during the development of the following successful HAE studies published during my time with the HAEA:

"Tolerability and Effectiveness of 17-α-Alkylated Androgen Therapy for Hereditary Angioedema: A Re-examination." June 2016, Article: Bruce L Zuraw, Donna K. Davis, Anthony J. Castaldo, Sandra C. Christiansen

Background: Hereditary angioedema (HAE) is a genetic disorder clinically characterized by recurrent attacks of subcutaneous and mucosal swelling. 17-α-Alkylated androgens (AA) have been used prophylactically to reduce HAE severity, but there are many questions about the efficacy and tolerability of AA. Objective: The objective of this study was to investigate the tolerability and effectiveness of AA therapy in a large cohort of patients with HAE. Methods: We performed a retrospective cross-sectional study on 650 subjects with HAE utilizing a one-time, anonymous, web-based survey. Based on an initial questionnaire, patients were routed to one of the following questionnaires: currently using AA, previously used but discontinued AA, or never used AA. Results: Statistical analysis revealed that androgens decreased attack frequency and severity in previous AA users (P < .0001) and current AA users (P < .0001). Substantial variability in the effectiveness was observed. Users who discontinued AA reported significantly lesser benefit. No dose effect was seen for the beneficial effect of AA; however, almost all users reported frequent side effects that were dose-related and often severe. Conclusions: AA therapy is usually effective for the treatment of HAE, although a substantial fraction of patients with HAE do not achieve adequate benefit. In contrast, the side effects of AA are seen in almost all subjects who take the medicines. If used, AA should only be recommended in the lowest effective and tolerated dose for carefully selected patients.

Pediatric Hereditary Angioedema: Onset, Diagnostic Delay, and Disease Severity

November 2015, Clinical Pediatrics: Sandra C. Christiansen, Donna K. Davis, Anthony J. Castaldo, Bruce L. Zuraw

Hereditary angioedema (HAE) typically presents in childhood. Large gaps remain in our understanding of the natural history of HAE during childhood. We examined age of onset, delay in diagnosis, androgen exposure, and their influence on ultimate disease severity in a large cohort of patients with HAE. Median age of first swelling was eleven years with a median age at diagnosis of nineteen years. Earlier onset of symptoms correlated with longer delays in diagnosis (P < .001) and predicted a more severe disease course, including increased number of attacks per year (P = .0009) and hospital admissions (P = .009). Earlier age of onset also significantly correlated with increased perceived HAE severity (P = .0002), negative overall life impact (P < .0001), and use of anabolic androgen. Our observations highlight the importance of early HAE diagnosis and suggest the necessity of a disease management plan once the diagnosis has been made.

Pediatric Presentation of Hereditary Angioedema (HAE) Due to C1 Inhibitor Deficiency

February 2013, Journal of Allergy and Clinical Immunology: Sandra C. Christiansen, Donna Davis, Anthony J. Castaldo, Bruce L. Zuraw

Several European surveys have reported that symptoms of HAE often begin in childhood. We sought to assess the age of symptom onset in a large population of United States HAE subjects and determine the implications of age of disease onset. METHODS: We performed an observational IRB approved study on adult subjects with HAE utilizing an anonymous, web-based survey. All subjects reported a history of physician-diagnosed HAE. Age of symptom onset, age of diagnosis, and attack frequency were assessed in 650 subjects. Symptoms of HAE began in the pediatric age range.

CONCLUSIONS: Our results confirm that HAE symptoms begin in childhood in the vast majority of patients, and further demonstrate that the severity of the disease as well as the delay in diagnosis are inversely associated with age of symptom onset. This study highlights the need for an enhanced focus on the diagnosis and management of HAE in children.

Million Miler

During the last years of the boys going to high school, their dad retired from the Hawaii Air National Guard and was hired by Aloha Airlines. Just as he was completing the probationary period with Aloha Airlines, the airline went bankrupt and then closed their business in 2008. My spouse was able to land on his feet through getting hired to provide flight simulator instruction to the Hawaii Air National Guard men and women. He was able to be with those he worked with for so many years prior. He was also finally able to have quality dad time with his boys and was on-island when I needed to travel for HAEA-related events and requirements.

During this time, the HAEA greatly expanded its services to HAE patients and to the many different HAE stakeholders. One of the most powerful and endearing experiences for HAE patients was to finally have the opportunity to meet up with other HAE patient families they had come to know and love through the HAEA social media community. The HAEA began hosting yearly HAE patient summits in a different part of the country each year. These summits also provided opportunities for HAE patients to learn from HAE physician experts and other stakeholders who would be developing patient access programs for newly approved HAE therapies. The HAEA patient services staff also began meeting with those who were developing the patient access programs for those newly approved HAE therapies. We helped them develop best practices from a patient perspective. I also continued to be involved in our ongoing advocacy on Capitol Hill. It did not take long for me to become a Million Miler with United Airlines with the many trips I made on and off the island.

The Slippery Slope of Divorce

My spouse and I married in 1983. We exchanged spiritual vows in the Lutheran church and were soulfully committed to each other. I truly believe that advocating for our son while continuing to take care of our day-to-day family needs fulfilled my marital vow. Sadly, and somewhat understandably, my spouse grew increasingly discontented as I and the HAEA continued to fight for access to therapy. My responsibilities kept growing as the vice president for patient services. I believe good old-fashioned upbringing and my spouse's personality made it difficult for him to cope with and accept the untraditional dynamics of what became of our family life. It gave me comfort to know he was trying to accept what was going on. The painful truth was, we were slipping into an exhausting cycle of him saying he supported and condoned my efforts and then displayed cycles of escalating anger toward the boys and me. It became clear to me that the most difficult part of the *very* challenging work I was doing was managing the turmoil at home. I wasn't aware of how bad things had gotten until my parents came to visit and said they had never in all their lives experienced such rudeness displayed by my spouse. They said they would not come back to stay with us in Hawaii. No amount of marital counseling could change our reality. In 2012, my spouse asked me what I saw our relationship to be like in the next five years. I told him that I wasn't sure, but I looked forward to the day when I wouldn't have to do all I was doing anymore and that we could do all the things we liked to do together again. Sadly, he responded with an ultimatum—a list of things that would have to change regarding our relations with each other, or "we" would be considering divorce.

I was heartbroken and dismayed when our divorce was finalized after twenty-nine years of marriage when I was fifty-one years old. There was little I could do to shield Kris from possibly thinking the divorce happened because he had HAE. I do believe both boys having grown accustomed to walking on eggshells when their dad was around did not attribute this family dynamic to my work for the HAEA.

I realized that landing on my feet would not be so easy! I knew the divorce would expose me to financial peril, but I had *no* idea what was to come. Most of the money I had made from working for the HAEA went toward the boys' expensive and necessary private school. I had no savings and no retirement from the many years of service to the association. The HAEA did not develop employee benefits until about two years before my separation with the organization. I did, however, qualify for 50 percent of the air force retirement awarded to my spouse, having been married for twenty-three years of his military service. What money I saved from the

HAEA 401K needed to be used to move myself off the island. There was no way I could afford to stay on the island. The boys had both graduated from high school and had already realized their independence. Both had robust social lives. Patrick and Kris told me they would prefer staying on the island, which was their home since early childhood. Their father had since gotten hired by Hawaiian Airlines and once again was off island quite often flying international routes as a newly hired second officer. The condominium on the nineteenth floor in Honolulu (1,200 square feet for four-plus people) which was supposed to be our starter home ended up being our much-too-small space for many years until it became the Davis men's bachelor quarters. I did tell both the boys I would try to help them relocate if ever they wanted to live in St. Louis. I moved back to St. Louis to be near my mom and my brother since I could not afford to stay on the island.

Moving Myself Off the Island

The income I was making with the association, the military retirement, and the condominium equity payout awarded to me from the divorce was sufficient to finance and sustain a home in St. Louis. I was able to buy a two-bedroom gingerbread cottage in the Southampton/South City area of St. Louis, Missouri. I made sure my mortgage payment would be no more than what I could pay with the military retirement money. Long before I could remember, our family befriended our next-door neighbor's family in St. Louis County. There were six kids in this devout Catholic home. My older brother, older sister, and I were the same age as three of the children in that family, and we remain friends today. Their family bought a bigger house in the Southampton/South City area of St. Louis when I was a teenager. Many of the homes in this area were ornate cottages, sometimes referred to as gingerbread cottages, constructed in the 1930s and '40s. I would do sleepovers in Southampton quite often with my friends at their new home in the summertime. We would run the neighborhood from morning until night. Some of the kids we ran with lived in these gingerbread cottages, and I got to see the insides of them. I never forgot the magic I felt while walking through the round, castle-like archways dividing the rooms. I marveled in the castle-like masonry on the outside of these cottages and the vibrant colors used in the stained-glass windows. I had fallen in love with these architecturally unique little masterpieces.

Missing My Boys

I missed the boys terribly and had to remind myself that empty-nest motherhood was inevitable at this time in my life. Kristian had become very good at doing his own infusions, and the specialty pharmacy in Hawaii that provided his medication took his continued access to supply very seriously. The pharmacy kept an extra month's supply in stock on-island for Kris in case of natural disaster or shipping interruptions. I was so thankful the Physician-Supervised Self-Managed C1 Inhibitor Replacement Therapy study was successful and allowed him to treat himself early, which really was lifesaving for him on a few occasions. I also felt good in knowing how close the boys had always been and that they would continue to watch out for each other. With access to this therapy in the home, Kristian's quality of life went from total disability to keeping himself attack-free. He was finally able to treat himself at first notice of his prodrome symptoms.[10] One of his prodrome

---

10   Prodrome, https://www.heretohelp.bc.ca/q-and-a/what-is-a-prodrome

symptoms was a rash that looked like a splotchy sunburn all over his body. The medical term for his rash that only 50 percent of the HAE patients experienced was "erythema marginatum."[11] He considered this part of HAE to be a blessing in knowing that an attack was about to happen, and it could be prevented. With all that said, I was going to be okay with not being on the island with Kris and Patrick.

---

11   https://www.dovemed.com/diseases-conditions/erythema-marginatum

Staying Strong for HAE and Me

I must admit, I did feel strong, even in the presence of another layer of adversity that was accumulating along this slippery slope. Part of having confidence in my strength was and still is my faith. Faith was keeping fear and anger at bay. Both would have been paralyzing for me.

Working in a virtual community came with both benefits and disadvantages. I made the decision not to make knowledge of my divorce public, which proved to be an advantage and disadvantage at the same time. I could not justify making a divorce announcement when not even the team I worked with knew if I was happily married or not. Had we all lived in one community, I would have felt differently. The privacy was beneficial for my confidence in the leadership role I was maintaining. If I had shared my experiences, I may have been spared from falling into the insidious, deep depression which I was unaware of at the time. Having a leadership role in the HAEA did come with a fairly high level of public exposure in the patient community. Visibility in the eyes of patients looking to the organization for strength was a huge responsibility and worthy of protection. I did not want knowledge of my divorce to create discouragement for patients who were already struggling so much in their own lives and families.

Life after FDA Approval

The patients in our community were overjoyed to finally not have to suffer through HAE attacks. However, many suffered from other medical conditions brought on by a lifetime of repeated HAE attacks. Because dental work (even cleaning) frequently triggered facial and laryngeal attacks, many patients chose not to have dental work done in fear of having a life-threatening attack. There were also patients in our community who had survived multiple heart attacks brought on by a lifetime of using anabolic steroids. Then there were HAE patients who emergency room staff referred to as the "drug seekers." Patients would repeatedly present to emergency departments with excruciatingly painful abdominal attacks. Typical diagnostic protocols did not account for HAE attacks, and patients were told there was nothing medically wrong with them. They were labeled drug seekers. Some chose to stop going in for medical care and would suffer through severe dehydration, hypotension, and bowel obstructions. Sadly, for those who were taken seriously, some did become dependent on prescription narcotic pain medications. Some patients could finally manage their HAE attacks but continued to struggle with drug dependency.

Chaitanya's Story

Chaitanya called into our emergency on-call line just after one of the medicines had been FDA approved. I was surprised to see a caller with an 808-area code, which was a Hawaii phone number. Based on population, statistically, there were only about fifty patients in all the Hawaiian Islands. A young lady's voice was on the other end, and she sounded afraid. She said, "You don't know me, but I know you through the Hereditary Angioedema Association." She said, "I know I have HAE by identifying my symptoms through internet research." She told me she had not been diagnosed. She said she had had symptoms throughout her teen years, but this was the first time to have throat swelling. I found out she was in the dormitory at the University of Hawaii just a few miles away. I knew we would have to act quickly. I could already hear the raspiness in her voice, which was common when a person's throat was swelling—stridor has a very distinct sound. I knew there was HAE therapy in the pharmacy at one of the smaller hospitals nearby on Oahu but none in the hospital she would be transported to from her dormitory. I also knew that she would more than likely not have access to that lifesaving treatment without a diagnosis. I could not convince Chaitanya to call 911, so I told her I would meet her at the small hospital that had the HAE medicine. She knew where it was. This was the first time I advocated for a patient other than Kris in person, and I wasn't sure how things would go. I got off the phone with Chaitanya and called and left a message for the doctor, who I knew had prescribed for and treated another patient with HAE. Kristian's hospital did not have the therapy, because he was infusing his treatments in the home. I was also able to find out that the pharmacy did currently have a supply of the therapy. I knew I would have to somehow convince the doctor in the emergency room to consider conducting a blood test for low levels of C4, which is almost always low during an HAE attack. Chaitanya, her adoptive mom Liz Perry, and I all arrived at the hospital within minutes of each other. I quickly introduced myself to Liz, and she encouraged me to do whatever I could to get Chaitanya diagnosed and treated. It was on this day that I realized how powerful a patient organization could be. Being a layperson, I half expected to get asked to leave by the medical staff. I explained who I was, and that the patient asked me to advocate on her behalf. I explained that I had already reached out to a staff physician at that hospital who treats another HAE patient, and that the pharmacy had a supply of the medicine Chaitanya would more than likely need to save her life but would need a diagnosis for that treatment. Much to my surprise, the C4 lab test was conducted, and she was diagnosed with HAE based on that preliminary test.

Chaitanya was able to get treated that day for the first time.

Kris and Chaitanya became fast friends. I was happy to know they ended up being there for each other in times of need during HAE attacks. Chaitanya and I also developed a close friendship. We communicated a lot about HAE, and I was surprised when she asked me many questions about being a mom and taking care of a family and home.

I learned that Chaitanya's biological mom and dad were nomadic hippies who roamed the Islands, and Chaitanya's upbringing was as far from normal as could be. She told me that at one time, the family lived in a teepee in the mountains. In her teen years, Chaitanya lived mostly with her father, which was not good for her. Chaitanya said that when she started more severe and frequent attacks of swelling, she reached out to a lady she had met and befriended through an at-risk youth program. Liz Perry, a realtor and community leader, donated her time to this youth program. As a member and instructor for an exclusive canoe club, the Outrigger Canoe Club, Liz would meet with and give surf lessons and outrigger canoe paddling lessons to these teenagers. Liz legally adopted Chaitanya and began giving her the care and attention she so desperately needed. Liz gave her a wonderful home and enrolled her in the La Pietra Hawaii School for Girls. Chaitanya graduated high school there and went on to become an honor student at Hawaii Pacific University. Chaitanya's inward beauty was just as striking as her beauty as a young woman. She had a magnetic personality. It did not take long for her to become a very successful HAE patient advocate and appear in the motion picture *Special Blood*.

With great sadness, I must also say that Chaitanya did struggle with dependence on the prescription narcotic pain medicines that were frequently prescribed when emergency room staff did take her excruciating pain seriously prior to her HAE diagnosis. Her body craved narcotics long after having access to HAE therapy. After Chaitanya's diagnosis, she got the help she needed to address her addiction and was given a pain management protocol for all medical caregivers to follow. In violation of the protocol, a physician allowed Chaitanya to go home post-surgery with a narcotic pain medicine prescription. Chaitanya passed away from an accidental overdose shortly after that surgery on August 2, 2014.

Debbie and Kris

Our president and physician advisors were able to convince pharmaceutical companies who did the clinical trials for HAE to provide compassionate emergency therapy once they began marketing their products. Compassionate doses were kept in the offices of physician who were treating other HAE patients with the newly marketed HAE therapies. The medicine could be used for those who did not have access to therapy while prescribed therapy plans were being set up.

An HAE patient, Debbie, who I had advocated for and known for many years, was vacationing with her husband on the neighboring island of Kauai. I got a call from Debbie around noon and learned that she had not gotten access to her HAE therapy prior to her vacation and was beginning to have symptoms of throat swelling. I asked her what her plan was. She said that she would have her husband drive her to the hospital to be intubated if needed. I told her I would call Kristian's doctor. Since Chaitanya's diagnosis event, Kristian's doctor began keeping compassionate C1 esterase inhibitor doses in his office through the compassionate therapy program. I called Dr. Bob, and he said, "If the patient could get on an interisland flight within the next hour and a half, she would be able to receive a compassionate treatment." Debbie and her husband *were* able to get on a flight. During the daytime, there were two to three flights between Kauai and Oahu every hour. The flights were only a half hour long. When I called Dr. Bob to let him know of Debbie's approximate arrival time at the hospital, he said it would take too long to get her admitted and told me to pick up the medicine and have Kris do the mixing and infusion for Debbie since he was trained by medical staff for his own therapy. The timing worked out *perfect*! I picked up the medicine, signed Kris out of his afternoon high school classes, and dropped him off at the condominium so he could begin preparing the infusion. I then headed to the airport and arrived just as the flight was landing. Debbie and her husband were both getting a little anxious on the ride to the condominium but felt better when they learned Kris had the infusion already prepared. We arrived, and Debbie, who was a nurse, asked Kris to start the IV and administer the medicine. Kris was the calmest one among us. The infusion was completed within ten minutes. Debbie began to feel better within minutes and said she did not think it was necessary to go to the emergency room for observation. They were able to fly back to Kauai on the last flight back to the island that evening. Kris told me later that this event and a couple other first-on-the-scene events he encountered made him realize he wanted to be a first responder.

HAEA Staff Battle Fatigue and Middle Management

To this day, I truly believe that every individual on the patient services team did consider their position a calling and served at the expense of their own needs and well-being. New responsibilities seemed to be mounting daily, and there was no foreseeable end to operating in "crisis mode." I realized battle fatigue was setting in as our staff continued to advocate. Pushback from insurance companies became our next battleground. The battle for access to medicine through insurance plans ensued upon the very first FDA-approved therapy becoming available. Insurance administrators do everything they can in order to not pay for the therapies HAE patients need to keep themselves safe.

My position in the organization fulfilled the role of middle management—a very difficult position in organizations with small numbers of staff numbers. In this situation, it is nearly impossible to keep communication above a personal level. The following quote sums up the challenge of my position in the HAEA as their middle manager:

"The hardship of being a middle manager…caught in the middle of top-level execs and the troops on the front lines, they've got to ace the balancing act. They are always juggling priorities, refereeing conflicts, and keeping the performance train on track while holding onto their sanity."[12] The combination of being a co-founder along with fulfilling the role of a middle manager proved to be quite a predicament and I believe accelerated me toward Founder's Syndrome. I was a middle manager for the HAEA because the association needed to have individuals with higher levels of education for the upper-level executive positions; I had not accomplished the higher level of education that was needed. The organization needed these higher levels of education in the executive staff in order to be credible in the eyes of medical and pharmaceutical industries and with the US government. I must admit, it was disappointing for me to be in a position in the organization to hire the executive vice president while not being eligible for that position. The roadblock to my education years earlier imposed by my spouse weighed heavy on me during this time.

---

12   https://www.icreatives.com/iblog/the-hardships-of-being-a-middle-manager-and-how-you-can-improve

The Perfect Storm: Stress, Sleep Deprivation, Battle Fatigue, Self-Medication, Founder's Syndrome, and Depression

Yes, a perfect storm was spinning up inside of me. The high-level, fight-or-flight stress was constant and escalating on all fronts in my life. Due to the twenty-four-hour nature of our business, my sleep deprivation consisted of only sleeping three to four hours at night and relying on fifteen-to-thirty-minute power naps to get through the days. I did not realize how quickly I was falling into a very deep depression from my sadness over the divorce, stress, and battle fatigue.

Chronic Fight-or-Flight Stress and Constant High Levels of Cortisol

Unfortunately, the ongoing high level of stress I had been experiencing for many years did predispose me to chronic high levels of cortisol, which did show up on laboratory testing I had done. Following is a good description of the severe effects chronic high cortisol levels can have on the body. I do believe my high cortisol level played a big role in me falling into a deep depression I did not realize was happening.

Chronic stress can wreak havoc on your mind and body. Take steps to control your stress.
By Mayo Clinic Staff

...Understanding the natural stress response—When you face a perceived threat, a tiny region at the brain's base, called the hypothalamus, sets off an alarm system in the body. An example of a perceived threat is a large dog barking at you during your morning walk. Through nerve and hormonal signals, this system prompts the adrenal glands, found atop the kidneys, to release a surge of hormones, such as adrenaline and cortisol.

Adrenaline makes the heart beat faster, causes blood pressure to go up, and gives you more energy. Cortisol, the primary stress hormone, increases sugar, also called glucose, in the bloodstream, enhances the brain's use of glucose, and increases the availability of substances in the body that repair tissues.

Cortisol also slows functions that would be nonessential or harmful in a fight-or-flight situation. It changes immune system responses and suppresses the digestive system, the reproductive system, and growth processes. This complex natural alarm system also communicates with the brain regions that control mood, motivation, and fear.

When the natural stress response goes wild—The body's stress response system is usually self-limiting. Once a perceived threat has passed, hormones return to typical levels. As adrenaline and cortisol levels drop, your heart rate and blood pressure return to typical levels. Other systems go back to their regular activities.

But when stressors are always present and you always feel under attack, that fight-or-flight reaction stays turned on.

The long-term activation of the stress response system and too much exposure to cortisol and other stress hormones can disrupt almost all the body's processes. This puts you at higher risk of many health problems: anxiety, depression, digestive problems, headaches, muscle tension and pain, heart disease, heart attack, high blood pressure and stroke, sleep problems, weight gain, [or] problems with memory and focus.[13]

Founder's Syndrome, Self-Medicating, and Depression

I have always enjoyed a nice-quality wine and developed a liking for beer after being exposed to the best beer in the world while living in Germany. I had a healthy relationship with alcohol. Sadly, due to the ever-increasing and overwhelming challenges of the association and the divorce, I did not realize at first that when everything was too much for me, I would "check out" by drinking more and more each time. I did not realize I was using alcohol to self-medicate; I was binge drinking to take away the pain.

---

13   https://www.mayoclinic.org/healthy-lifestyle/stress-management/in-depth/stress/art-20046037

While on a business trip with the entire staff, I was terribly upset at how things were going with what had become a toxic work environment. I was becoming exhausted from managing conflicts among our staff. I was spending just about all of my time addressing staff issues in the midst of still operating in crisis mode for our patient community. I was ultimately responsible for our work environment in my supervisory position. Everything was coming to a head during this weekend meeting. I proceeded into an alcoholic binge at the hotel bar in the presence of some of the staff members. Sadly, I do not remember what I said, but I'm sure it was no-holds-barred in expressing my frustration. The president called me the next morning, during which time I told him I thought I should probably resign. He said, "I'm glad you said that, because if not, I would have had to tell you that you must resign." I did resign. Sadly, I did not know I was in the throes of Founder's Syndrome.

Following is a very good discussion about Founder's Syndrome. Oh, how I wish had known to guard against this phenomenon:

What Is Founder's Syndrome—The Nutshell Version

Founder's Syndrome occurs when a single individual or a small group of individuals bring an organization through tough times (a start-up, a growth spurt, a financial collapse, etc.). Often these sorts of situations require a strong, passionate personality—someone who can make fast decisions and motivate people to action.

Once those rough times are over, however, the decision-making needs of the organization change, requiring mechanisms for shared responsibility and authority. It is when those decision-making mechanisms don't change, regardless of growth and changes on the program side, that Founder's Syndrome becomes an issue. We see this most frequently with organizations that have grown from a mom-and-pop operation to a $12 million community powerhouse, while decisions are still made as if the founders are gathered around someone's living room, desperately trying to hold things together.

What Founders Need to Know

We use two analogies to describe our relationship to the organization we founded. We try not to mix these metaphors, but sometimes it happens. Here goes:

Once you have birthed it, it is no longer your baby. Just as it is with our own children, once they are born, they are their own persons. We can guide our children, teach them, nurture them—but our son or daughter is a person in his/her own right. As is "our" organization. It's not ours. It is its own thing. We don't own it.

Once you give a gift, it's no longer yours. Okay—that's the other metaphor. We have created this amazing gift for our community. Now that it is used and depended upon by others, now that we have given this gift to the community, it is no longer ours. It belongs to the community. That's the definition of a gift.

From these two facts—that the organization is a being in its own right and that that being belongs to the community, not us—come a number of other facts many founders don't want to face.

1) Along with the decision to bring a child into the world comes the responsibility to raise it to live independently. We all know the old adage—that the only certainties in life are death and taxes. Well, the part we don't like to admit to ourselves is that there is another certainty associated with the "death" part—and that is that none of us knows exactly when our days will be done. Because we know we are not going to live forever, and we cannot know if our last day will be tomorrow or fifty years from now, it is irresponsible to run our organizations as if we will, in fact, be around forever. It is simply not fair to the organization, nor to those who benefit from the work we do. The only responsible approach, therefore, is to raise this child to NOT need us.

2) The world doesn't owe you anything for having founded your organization. We gave up our lives to create the organization we founded. We went without sleep, sweated blood, and in our case, even went into debt. But the sad truth is that nobody owes us anything for doing that. We did it because we cared. And regardless of which metaphor you use—that of having a child, or that of giving a gift—neither of them provides for a payback. Our "payback" in having a child is in seeing our children grow and take on the world themselves. And our "payback" for giving a gift is in seeing how happy the

recipient is to use that gift, hopefully for a long, long time.

3) It's not about you. Harsh, but true. It's hard sometimes to acknowledge that regardless of how much we put into nurturing the organization we founded, in the long run, none of that really matters. It's not about our emotional needs—regardless of what those are. It's not about what we've sacrificed to make it all work, or the recognition/gratitude we think we should get. It's about the community, which is why we created this gift in the first place. If we have not prepared the organization to survive (and dare I say thrive?) without our presence, and we therefore cannot even think of leaving, as the organization would crumble without us, then we have somehow made it about us rather than about the community.

4) Your vision isn't nearly as important as the organization's vision and the community's vision. Yes, it was our vision that founded the organization in the first place. But as the organization grows and matures, that vision may not be all there is. The ability for the organization to dramatically affect the community may be far larger than the vision we had when we first opened the doors...[14]

Insidious Depression and Denial

---

[14] https://help4nonprofits.com/NP_Bd_FoundersSyndrome_Art.htm

The overwhelmingly high levels of stress, sleep deprivation, and sadness and the physiological effects of high cortisol led me to a subconscious denial of the deep depression I had fallen into. I needed to stay strong. High cortisol levels and depression share the same symptoms. I do believe the side effects of both, which I call the Perfect Storm, resulted in the catastrophic event at the staff meeting that ended my service to the HAEA and probably saved my life.

Understanding Denial and Its Role in Mental Health — Defining Denial: A Psychological Perspective

"Psychologists view denial as a defense mechanism that distorts reality to shield individuals from threatening or overwhelming situations. It acts as a protective shield, allowing individuals to maintain a semblance of control and stability in the face of uncertainty or distress.

When individuals engage in denial, they create a psychological barrier that shields them from the pain and discomfort associated with facing difficult emotions or experiences.

Denial as a Defense Mechanism

As a defense mechanism, denial allows individuals to shield themselves from painful emotions and threatening situations. By denying the existence or severity of depression, individuals may temporarily alleviate anxiety and stress, enabling them to function in day-to-day life. However, this protective mechanism can prevent individuals from seeking necessary support and hinder their journey toward recovery and emotional well-being.

The Psychological and Physical Impact of Depression

Depression not only affects an individual's mental well-being but also has considerable physical and cognitive repercussions. Chronic fatigue, body aches, headaches, digestive issues, and impaired memory or concentration are common manifestations of depression. The overarching impact of depression extends beyond the individual, affecting relationships, work performance, and overall functioning in various domains of life.

How Denial Manifests in Depressed Individuals

Depressed individuals often find themselves downplaying their symptoms or attributing them to other causes such as stress, tiredness, or a temporary mood fluctuation. Denial may manifest as a defense mechanism against acknowledging the true extent of their emotional pain, discrediting the seriousness of their condition, or disguising their struggles from others.[15]

---

15 https://drhandoo.com/is-denial-a-sign-of-depression/

Healing from Depression — Storm Cleanup

Thankfully, I was given severance pay following my resignation and the end of my service to the HAEA. I did take time to make doctor appointments to address my health issues. In reaching out for help to address my poor sleep habits, I also learned how deeply I had fallen into severe depression. Between the severance pay money and the military retirement medical benefits, I was able to spend the next several months to get the care I needed. Picking up the pieces was a skill I had refined all throughout my adult life, and I did hold on to the confidence in my ability to help myself. The professional help I received continues to empower me to live a life free from depression and free from any form of substance abuse.

Life After Serving the HAEA

It did not take long for me to become painfully aware of the need to sell the gingerbread cottage. I had joyfully and systematically restored what needed to be restored in the house during the few years I lived there. Yes, I was able to afford the mortgage on my military retirement, but I was not able to put any money away to keep the house from falling into disrepair. Without the HAEA income, I would have to sell the property before any costly repairs became necessary. I needed to sell the house while it was still in good marketable shape. The house sold within one week of being on the market, and I became a renter. This turned out to be a decision I wished I *never* had to make. I knew that being a renter was an inherent insecurity, and sure enough, it would prove to be a disaster for me. The loss of income coming in from the HAEA spiraled me into financial peril, and the next three turns of events landed me at the bottom of that slippery slope.

For about the last year of work and travel for the HAEA, I was developing some progressive and pretty severe pain in the knee that was reconstructed twelve years prior. As predicted when I had my knee reconstruction surgery, arthritis would eventually set in. Sure enough, it had. After exhausting all other methods to relieve the debilitating pain, I agreed to a partial knee replacement. The surgery and rehabilitation went well, and I was back on my feet and fully functioning within two months. A year and two weeks after that surgery, the partial knee replacement failed. The prosthetic broke loose and caused a fracture. Much to my dismay, I learned that replacing an already-replaced knee, which is called revision knee replacement, could only be done by a specially trained orthopedic specialist. The fracture occurred in July, and I hobbled on crutches until January of the next year, which was the first available opening for this type of surgery. Once again, the surgery went well, and I was able to achieve full recovery and functionality.

During this time, I tried my hand at freelance patient advocacy. I was able to do some month-to-month contract work for the HAEA, which really helped out during my recovery. I worked with the new senior executive vice president of the HAEA who was hired to take the association to the next level. I hoped the next level continued to be good for the patient community.

Reinventing Myself

As much as I would have liked, there was no way I could live on just the military retirement money, which equated to half a military retirement. I knew there was nothing I could do to bring in the amount of money I earned during my time with the HAEA. I could not even come close. Age, not being able to advance in higher levels of a college degree and working in such a niche role for most of my adult life really required me to be creative while trying to break into a new vocation. Healthcare? First responder? Law enforcement? Who would ever start a new career at the age of fifty-three? ME! My first step was to start combing through the Indeed job website to see what kind of jobs were being advertised. Jobs in law enforcement and healthcare stood out. As a layperson (not medically trained), I would only qualify for entry-level positions in a hospital. An entry-level position would not be sufficient to carry myself through to retirement. I realized that not only Kris, but I, too, would be a good first responder. Most law enforcement positions required prior military service or previous experience in an armed position. I did not have either. I did, however, see that Loomis Armored, LLC, was hiring for armed driving positions that offered the arms training to new hires. Upon inquiring, I was hired right away. I had already gone through conceal and carry and defensive handgun training and maintained a conceal and carry license. I really enjoyed this new position. The pay was good enough to carry me while I accrued the experience needed to hopefully qualify for a government or state law enforcement position that would give a good retirement.

COVID and COVID Pneumonia

Just three months after I started actively driving for Loomis, I developed a mild dry cough a half hour into my route. By the end of the day, I could not stop coughing and was developing breathing difficulty. My crew and I had to abort the route early. From the Loomis building, I drove directly to the emergency room. I was diagnosed with COVID. By the next morning, my breathing had gotten much worse, so I went back to the hospital where I was diagnosed. I was admitted for low oxygen saturation levels. I had COVID pneumonia. Two hospital stays and one month later, I was able to return to work. Loomis had just changed their sick leave/vacation policy. Everyone was given thirty days a year to be use for sick leave and vacation time, called paid time off (PTO). I had COVID pneumonia the entire month of January and had no PTO left upon my return. It was necessary for me to keep my follow-up appointments and respiratory therapy appointments. Sadly, I had not been with the company long enough to qualify for temporary disability. I asked the human resources department what would happen if I took more time off for medical appointments and was told I would start on a disciplinary action track. The third absence before the end of the year would result in termination. I resigned. I was not going to let Loomis tarnish my work record with a termination. I was out of work *again*! It did not take long for me to run out of money. I had to decide between making my car payment or paying the rent. I thought *surely* the apartment management would be willing to work with me. I had already started looking for employment and was in negotiations for a position with a health insurance company. My plan was to make partial rent payments for two months and then pay back the balance owed once I got hired. This was during the time when everyone was in lockdown for COVID. The apartment management office was not open, and no one would return my many calls or online requests. I did not have the money to make the past-due rent payments along with the current rent payment. There was NO way to make partial payments online, which was the only way rent payments could be made. The rental office was in the adjacent property owned and run by the same corporation. I did not have access to that property due to the COVID lockdown. I was, however, able to access the building behind another resident and found a rental office staff member in the office. I explained what was going on and was told the corporate accountant would be giving me a call. I waited another month with no ability to make a partial payment. I even started to receive delinquency notices, which I'm sure were automated. The good news was, I began my training to work in the call center for the healthcare insurance company. In fear of my debt compounding, I decided to put my things in storage and move out of the apartment. I informed the property manager by email that I had vacated. I could not let the rent payment problem continue to go on. I knew that my dear friend Carol Dotson—yes, Carol from the second grade—rented the second master suite of their home to transient missionaries. So, I called her to see if she had a vacancy. She did! I was so fortunate to be able to move in with my friend until I could get situated in another apartment.

As I settled into my medical insurance call center position, which paid the bills, I continued to research educational, law enforcement, and government work opportunities. I was also able to get into another apartment within five months, and it was good to have a place to call my own again. During my routine trolling of the job market, a position was being offered that seemed to have been written for me! A hospital location which was located less than a mile from my new apartment was hiring for armed security guard positions. The hospital was in the process of hiring and training additional officers for newly established weapon detection checkpoints and overall hospital security. After submitting my application, resume, and cover letter that highlighted my experience in patient advocacy, first responding, and de-escalation skills, I was granted a virtual interview within a day. The very next day, I was given an offer letter. My six-week Public Safety Officer Training Academy (the hospital's police academy) class date was scheduled for two months out. I started my in-house training in the hospital a week after I was hired. Success! I was hired at a higher level of starting pay in recognition of my extensive medical community background. I would receive medical benefits and would be given a small pension after five years of service.

Living in the Giving

He was right. I agree. My mentor, the president of the HAEA, said, "Nobody really cares about what we did."

My experience is just how it was written in the details I shared regarding Founder's Syndrome. The world doesn't owe us anything for having founded our organization. We gave up our lives to create the organization we founded. We went without sleep, sweated blood, and in our case, even went into debt. But the sad truth is that nobody owes us anything for doing that. We did it because we cared.

I struggle financially, and my looming retirement years are full of uncertainty. I find great peace in knowing all I can do now is what I can with what I have. My happiness is in knowing patients are now *safe* so long as they have access to therapy and a good quality of life.

Every night, darkness comes. Darkness is necessary. But just as darkness comes, the sun rises to expose breathtaking beauty, good, and happiness. I see and know this when I realize the health and happiness of my two amazing sons. I see and know this in the countless accounts of success in the lives of over 10,000

HAE patients. I see and know this with each new scientific and medical advancement for this orphan disease, hereditary angioedema. HAE patients currently have nine FDA approved therapies and there are currently four ongoing clinical trials to study new scientific approaches for managing HAE here in the US.

> If you're black, if you're white, if you're weird, baby we're born that way. 'Cause I've got five cards, you've got yours, I've got mine. Five cards. Give me a hand this time!
>
> — *"House Always Wins" lyrics by Taj Farrant*

HAE: A Historical Perspective

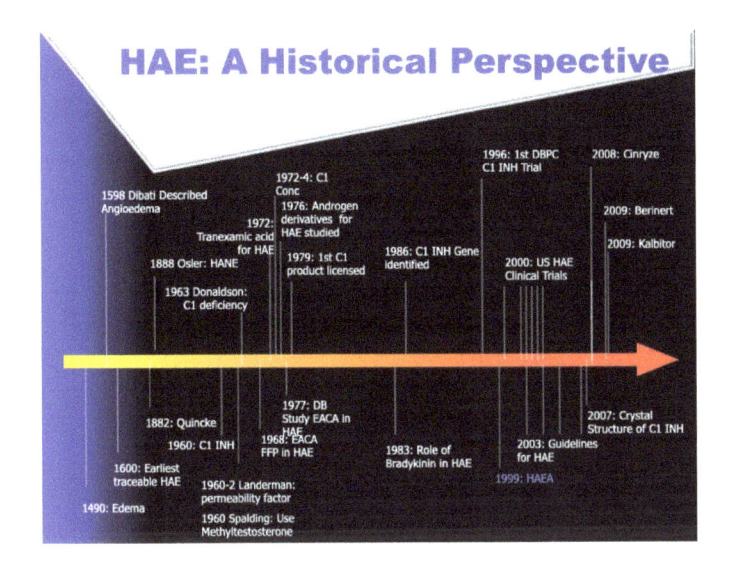

Above the timeline:
- 1598 Dibati Described Angioedema
- 1888 Osler: HANE
- 1963 Donaldson: C1 deficiency
- 1972: Tranexamic acid for HAE
- 1972-4: C1 Conc
- 1976: Androgen derivatives for HAE studied
- 1979: 1st C1 product licensed
- 1986: C1 INH Gene identified
- 1996: 1st DBPC C1 INH Trial
- 2000: US HAE Clinical Trials
- 2008: Cinryze
- 2009: Berinert
- 2009: Kalbitor

Below the timeline:
- 1490: Edema
- 1600: Earliest traceable HAE
- 1882: Quincke
- 1960: C1 INH
- 1960-2 Landerman: permeability factor
- 1960 Spalding: Use Methyltestosterone
- 1968: EACA FFP in HAE
- 1977: DB Study EACA in HAE
- 1983: Role of Bradykinin in HAE
- 1999: HAEA
- 2003: Guidelines for HAE
- 2007: Crystal Structure of C1 INH

In 1999, the US Hereditary Angioedema Association organizes to accelerate HAE patient access to lifesaving therapies for treating and preventing attacks of Hereditary Angioedema. Slide provided by Dr. Henry Li.

Milton Keynes UK
Ingram Content Group UK Ltd.
UKHW021848231024
450082UK00009B/487